For Gregory, Barbara and Natasha

All those images that became alive under your eyes are for you.
Can you hear the nightingale, the purple sky, the jaguar, the fly?
Sound just came out of paper, it's magic, just like you!

an
alphabet
in
bloom

Nathalie Trovato

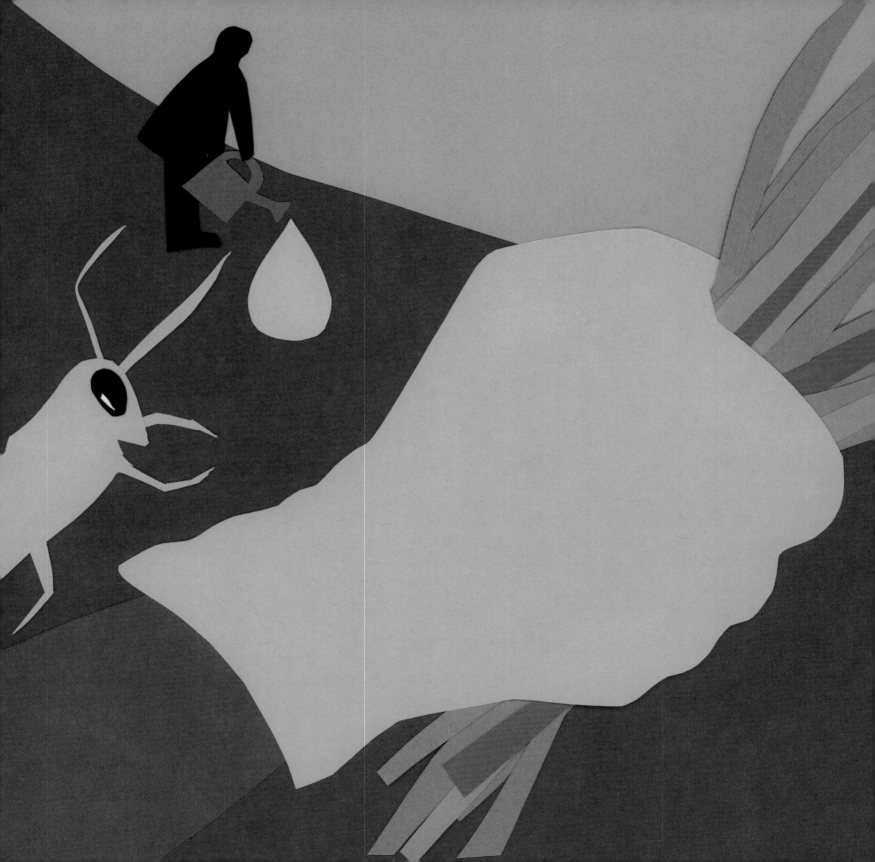

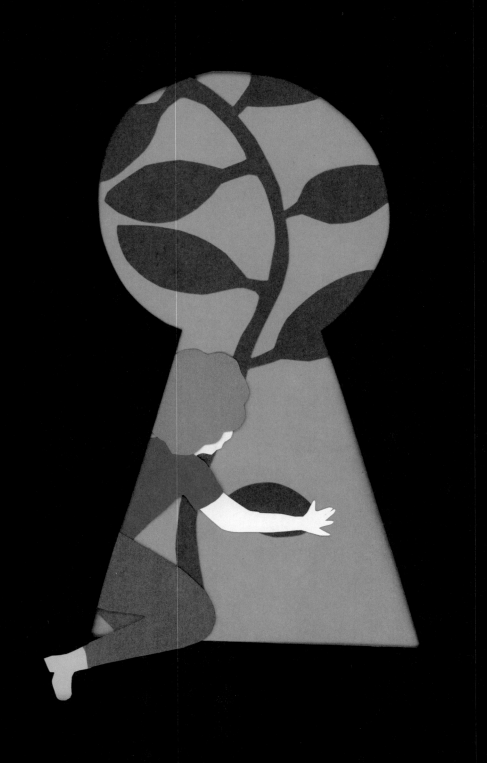

What can you see from a to z?

alive	fly	iris	oval	trunk
ant	foliage	ivy	parrot	tulips
antennae	food	jaguar	petal	twig
apple	four	jasmine	pistil	two
beak	frog	julia butterfly	pollen	umbrella plant
bird	garden	jungle	poppy	under
birdhouse	gardener	keyhole	pupil	venus flytrap
bloom	giant	kid	purple	vicious
blossom	glove	knee	quail	violet ground beetle
blue	grab	kneel	queen anne's lace	waste
breezy	grass	ladder	quiet	watering can
caterpillar	grasshopper	ladybug	rabbit	weeds
chlorophyll	green	leaves	raindrops	wheel
crawl	grow	look	rose	wheelbarrow
creeping	hair	moon	run	wilting
daffodil	hand	mosquito	sand	work
dawn	head	mound	seeds	xenops
dew	herbs	mushroom	shovel	(e)xamine
dragonfly	hill	nature	six	(e)xplorer
droop	hold	nest	snail	yard
droplets	horizon	night	soil	yellow cosmos
dusk	hose	nightingale	spade	yellow jacket
eat	hug	nine	spider	yorkie
edible	hummingbird	olives	spiral	zebra butterfly
eight	insect	onion	spun	zigzag
entrée	inside	orange	three	zucchini
fence	inspect	oregano	tree	

Nathalie Trovato is a French artist, educator and polyglot
who lives in Brooklyn with her inspirational family.
She considers herself a visual translator and through her
minimalist approach she creates poetic connections
between words and images.

Home Grown Books® is a registered trademark.

Designed by Cari Sekendur & Louis de Villiers
Art Directed by Jessica Brown
Manufactured in Rhode Island, USA
Meridian Printing
May 2017

Printed on recycled paper using certified wind power energy and
vegetable based inks with low-VOC. All materials used are acid free,
FSC and SFI Certified.

Published by Home Grown Books
homegrownbooksnyc.com

ISBN 978-0-9970587-2-7

First Edition